MW01093132

YOU DON'T KNOW JACK

(A TRUE STORY OF STATE CORRUPTION AS
EXPERIENCED BY INMATE M3356)

After surviving a year and a half in jail and four years in prison, I was released and set free, thanks to one man that put his career on the line. These are his words.

RICHARD H. SCHMACK
State's Attorney

"I truly wish that this crime had been solved, and her true killer were incarcerated for life. When I began this lengthy review, I had expected to find some reliable evidence that the right man had been convicted. No such evidence could be discovered.

Compounding the tragedy by convicting the wrong man, and fighting further in the hopes of keeping him jailed, is not the proper legacy for our community or for the memory of Maria Ridulph."

Conclusion

"It is a manifest impossibility for (Jack McCullough) to have been in Sycamore at 6:45 and also have made a phone call in downtown Rockford at 6:57."

Dedication

There are so many people that contributed to my journey through this incredible saga. Each person had a crucial part to play in getting me out of prison. They took risks that could have and, in fact, did endanger their jobs. The palace intrigue would also make an interesting story. All of the people involved in aligning the path to get me free are incredible personalities that dared fight the powers aligned against me. I dedicate this book to them in the hope that others will dare to step up when justice is needed.

CHAPTER ONE
ALMOST

My name is Jack Daniel McCullough. I, as an individual, am not important to the story you are about to read. What happened to me is important. The States of Illinois and Washington will wish that they had never heard of me. At the time of this writing, the residents of both states are in jeopardy because some of the people in law enforcement and the judicial officers still have their jobs after they put me in prison for something they knew I did not do.

In this story you will see the unchecked power of state employees. They almost got away with a crime except for the presence of some brave and determined people that fought for me and obtained my freedom. The good guys in this story came forward of their own volition, knowing that they could lose their jobs for doing the right thing.

This is not a minor story about corruption and injustice, it is a MAJOR story about corruption and injustice. I lost my freedom for five and a half years. There have been many media stories about this case and a few books written as well. One of the books, Piggyback, by Jeffrey Dean Doty, may have saved my life. The best media story is by CNN's Ann O'Neill on the internet.

In this book, I will also tell you some of the things that I learned about prison that could help the average inmate or innocent victim of Illinois corruption.

This was to be the oldest cold case in American History ever successfully prosecuted. It was all of that except for one small error: It was all a lie and they knew it. They were going to get me killed and they were going to be famous. It almost worked.

CHAPTER TWO
INCARCERATION

My story has already been written. The first and best book about my case is Piggyback by Jeffrey Dean Doty. I am free, after five and a half years in prison for a crime I did not commit. I am not important, but what happened to me is. It takes place in Seattle, Washington and Sycamore, Illinois. This is a small part of the story through my eyes. The following is meant to inform both the innocent and the guilty of what to expect after the conviction.

When the judge pronounced me guilty of kidnap and murder, the crowded courtroom burst into cheers. Everyone was on their feet hugging and celebrating. This was real, I was officially a convicted child killer. I was also a former police officer. Those are two things you do not want to be in prison. Keep in mind that I was innocent and had the proof in a box on the table. To my astonishment, the prosecution asked the judge to ban the FBI documents and the judge agreed. I knew at that moment that I was going to prison. I should have jumped up and asked the judge if he had ever read the Constitution. I had passed a polygraph test and could prove my location. I was on the phone with my stepfather at the exact time of the kidnapping. The FBI verified that the call was made. What more did I need?

Truth and justice apparently doesn't matter in Illinois. It took me four years to get before a judge again and this time I had a friend in the court, State's Attorney Richard Schmack, a brave and honorable man. He did months of reading and research and came to the conclusion that set me free.

After an estimated one hundred people spilled out of the courtroom, I was taken out of the courthouse under heavy guard for my protection. All hallways were blocked to hide my exit. I was driven to the jail and released to my cell pod where I sought counsel from an inmate that had been in several of the Illinois prisons. The first thing he said was, "Don't worry, it's no big deal", which was somewhat comforting to a convicted child killer and former police officer. He told me that I would need about six hundred dollars to get set up and have some necessities that would get me through the discomfort of prison life. It turns out he was right, but it would be months before I would make contact with my wife. The administration told lies to my wife and treated her rudely. She was told that I could call at any time, leaving her with the belief that I didn't want to talk to her. In truth, they withheld my phone code that would let me make any calls, so she was at home crying and feeling abandoned. I found that relatives were not treated with respect, and I was angry. My wife was not guilty of anything, and this was not the only time she was treated this way. After two months inside, I finally made the first call to her. My news was of little comfort to her. I was in the worst prison that Illinois had, with often cruel male guards and beautiful female guards.

I would need her help for years to come. I chose well when I married her; she would stand by me for the next five and a half years.

The most important purchase was a 13-inch flat screen TV which would be my contact with the outside world.

I spent about fifty dollars a month on treats and necessities like toiletries. My wife sent me books through Amazon. I studied both Japanese and Chinese writing. I was determined not to waste my time. I would treat this incarceration as if I were in a monastery and I was here to learn. I knew that if I could get an appearance before a judge and get someone to read the FBI documents, I would be released. All I needed to do was survive until that day came.

CHAPTER THREE
IMPACT

The impact of the false arrest in Seattle was unbelievably devastating on me, my wife, and all of her family. When exactly did the laws change that allowed any Public Servant to lie to the people they work for? They wanted me to drive my truck to the Seattle Police Department, so they could impound and search it after they arrested me. (Reader take note)

The next day I told my wife that I knew that they were not telling the truth, so I would force them to play the next card. I was right, because they came back with guns drawn. No arrest warrant and no authority, only the word of an Illinois State Trooper. I was not yet formally arrested, just detained and held for interrogation by several detectives that ignored all of my Constitutional rights. (See Fifth Amendment Note) I worked nights as a security guard for the residents of a thirty-two story building. I had not slept since the day before. Meanwhile, my wife was being lied to and asked to open our gun safe. It couldn't have been a legal search because they didn't know I had it, I had just purchased it three days prior. They searched my legal papers and noted the amount of guns and ammunition. I was legal, they were not. Washington State recognizes the Second Amendment. Illinois, not so much.

My last statement to the trooper was, "Either arrest me or let me go." That is when Seattle's problems began. I was going to the King County Jail on an Illinois arrest. Because I'd had a heart operation, I am on medication for life. I advised the staff when I was booked and I told every officer that I came in contact with.

I told them to talk to my wife, which they did. The clock was ticking and they were making demands, slowing down the process.

When my blood pressure reached 205/130, Medic One and a nice EMT calmed me down and gave me oxygen. Intensive care is just that, intensive. My wife learned of my situation on the news.

Mine was to be the oldest cold case successfully prosecuted in American history. High five.

If an inquisitive person from the judge's office wants to question you, refuse the interview. I foolishly responded negatively and paid for it later. She asked me, "What gives you stress?" Somewhat jokingly I responded, "Blacks, Muslims, and Democrats." Guess who my cellmates turned out to be? Yep, all of the above. One cellie was a Black Muslim Democrat. My first cellie was a Jew-hating Palestinian. This judge wanted me to suffer more than just going to prison. He wanted me dead and would have given me the death penalty. Thankfully that penalty does not exist in Illinois.

Wherever you are assigned, when you arrive, the guards will want to see you naked. They will tell you to move your privates this way and that, bend over and spread your cheeks, squat, and cough before you shower. Next comes clothing, bedding, basic toiletries and two boxes, one large and one small. They will be with you always, one is for most everything that will fit. The other is for your legal documents and that means documents only. Guards usually leave the small box alone while they are in your cell. I found out later that they do read everything that they can get their hands on. You have no control over where it goes when you are not present. You will find that all thieves are not on your side of the bars and things of value disappear often. It won't do any good to complain.

CHAPTER FOUR
INCOMING

Your life's caprice begins when you enter the processing center, where decisions are made that will determine your future. This is where you will be screened for medical, mental and threat status. The nature of your crime will be a factor in which prison you will be shipped to. Expect your stay to be days, if not weeks.

Next is a bus ride, and mine took seven hours, handcuffed to a chain that ran down the length of the bus between us. Prison buses have small windows near the roof line, and all you will see is sky and telephone poles. The restroom was a bucket in the back.

I was destined for the maximum security prison at Menard. Menard's first guests were from the Civil War, so it could be classified as dungeon-like and was so cold, I sometimes slept fully clothed.

In the three months that I was there, three inmates were killed by their cellmates. Two guards and a pastor were beaten so badly that one needed facial reconstruction. This was at church! In my opinion, Menard needs to be closed, torn down, and rebuilt. I would fire everyone and start over with experienced guards from other prisons, because the attitude of the guards was antagonistic. The administrative folks were fine.

Most of the inmates used a nickname, and some were quite creative, like my cellmate that chose to be called "Mister." I thought that to be clever because few would know his real name but most would remember "Mister". He was the one that helped me learn to write and read Arabic, and for that I am grateful.

Cellmate assignments are not always logical and can be deadly. Inmates that choose their celli, for whatever reason, seem to have the best result. Some live together for years with few problems.

CHAPTER FIVE
POWER

When riding on the prison bus, handcuffed to the chain, you are not thinking about the power that you may have, but let me give you something to ponder: What does any government entity fear? Exposure that reveals incompetence and a wide variety of things that could cost them their jobs or pensions. What is your power? I'll just speak from my own experience. My power was that I had media attention and a heart condition. You will see later how that played out. It was state corruption that put me on that bus to Menard Prison and it was anger that made me focus my energies and resolve to be free. That resolve kept me going. I had a strong and devoted wife that would stand by me for five and a half years. I also had powerful people that gave me hope and kept me alive. You will meet them later in the book. The fact that I am writing this book from my residence in Seattle is proof of power.

Each of you has your own story to tell, so tell it to whomever will listen. Buy pads of yellow lined paper and start writing.

CAPTER SIX
NOISE

For a few days after my arrival at Menard Prison, I was in the general population. The time I spent there was an awakening to just how on the edge we are to a societal breakdown. The noise level is almost painful. Yes, it is a racial thing. Don't fight it, you won't win.

Thankfully I am a little hard of hearing. I would have been grateful to be deaf. In a situation like this, I would chew up some paper and fit it in my ear canal. Once it dries, it will maintain its shape for a long time.

In Vietnam, on a firebase we were always in close proximity to mortars or artillery so I kept my hearing, though somewhat diminished, with paper plugs.

Once you are given the opportunity to shop in the commissary, you can buy earplugs. The best earplugs are created when your earbuds for your TV quit functioning. Just cut off the wire with the plug

I knew that if I could get before a judge and get someone to read the FBI documents, I would be released. All I needed to do was survive until that day came (Four years later).

As you will learn later in this book, language knowledge actually opened doors and kept me safe in some instances. I gained some respect from Muslims because I could read Arabic.

CHAPTER SEVEN
CELLIE

One thing the newly convicted must learn is the rules. I call it cell etiquette. If you don't get these unwritten rules, you could suffer serious consequences from the guy most likely to kill you, your cellie (cellmate). For example, some cells are only four and a half to five feet wide. If you need to pass a standing cellie sideways, do so back to back. Usually, only one person will have the floor, the sink, or the toilet. The other guy will stay on his bed. Don't complain if you get the top bunk because the bottom bunk is usually reserved for the old, the injured, or the meanest guy. Most cells are eleven feet long and contain a bunk (flat steel plate) and two shelves. When they are in use, you will wait your turn.

When the toilet is in use, you will face the wall or the bars. The underside of the seat is splashed with very cold water. Every time you flush it is ice cold and you will have to flush often so that you don't offend your cellie. If you just need to pass gas, get on the toilet and flush after each emission. Failure could lead to a fight. If it comes to a fight, your next destination is SEG (segregation).

Treat your cellie with respect and find things in common. Avoid conflict if you can.

CHAPTER EIGHT
END DATE

Except for lifers, many have an attainable "End Date." My end date was my last breath. I was a dead man awaiting murder by my cellmate. It would happen as I slept. All of my cellmates were murderers, except one; a molester that I felt safe with.

I was not ready for my amazing release by an incredibly courageous Prosecutor that gave up his career for me. Little did the voting public know, they had just UN-elected the only man in Illinois history that would come to their aide if they were innocent. When you, the reader, are finished reading this book, you must find a way to reward this man and any others like him.

The America that I was so proud of has been destroyed by people that think with their feelings and not with their brains. The brightest bravest people in our political history were the Founding Fathers. Few people can compare and yet most think that they know better. Finally the people have spoken but it took the election of a foreign agent to wake the American people up (IMHO). Your end date requires preparation. Don't walk out the gate broke and friendless or you will be right back in jail after a year or so. You know how to make money, so do it. Some of the smartest people I have ever met are inside the walls. You just need to go to the library to find them.

CHAPTER NINE
FEAR

Part of growing up has to deal with fear. Controlling fear is necessary so you don't expose your feeling of vulnerability. The best thing that can help to control that is earning your cell mate's respect and forming a bond. If you look out for each other, you may sleep better. Make as many of these bonds as you can, but especially take care of your cellie. Just so you don't get too comfortable; if you are going to get killed, it will most likely be your cellie that does it.

Be very aware whenever you are going anywhere. There will never be enough guards to see everything, so keep your hand near the rail when going down stairwells (in the event that you are pushed). Watch your back when you reach a landing because these areas offer a chance for mischief. This is where you get blindsided. You will be out cold and no one will come to your aid.

An attack can happen anywhere and at any time and it doesn't have to be out of sight. Men have been stabbed in plain sight on the yard. It is common practice for bad guys to hide a blade in the dirt on the yard.

Every prison is going to be different than the next. If you stay out of trouble, you could end up in a minimum security prison. It may have some perks that are appealing but the rule makers can screw that up.

Speaking of rules, the inmates have a few more unwritten rules that you should learn and heed. For example: the phone is the link to the loved ones. Sometimes it is difficult to get to a phone. Plan ahead and get to the phone first. It isn't the end of the world so don't make a big deal of it. If you see a phone just hanging, it has been claimed so leave it alone unless you are prepared to fight and perhaps die.

I may be painting a dark picture and I may be instilling more fear so I will also tell you that there are good times. You will laugh, watch a lot of TV, cheer on your team, and eat some really good burritos made by the guy next door. You will have the opportunity to get a first class education if you have the discipline.

CHAPTER TEN
SOLUTIONS

States' financial problems began in 1960 when liberalism took root in the educational system and made Socialism popular to the point of anarchy. Thanks to you, the voter, for finally coming to the rescue and UN-electing so many liberals. Now I offer the real culprit and that is the Unions that suck the life's blood out of every state and put the least qualified in charge of your children's minds.

. Their goal is to dumb down the population so that they are easy to control and rob. The shame is that they and the Unions were once more conservative and at least pretended to be patriotic. The Union that has invaded government should never have been given access to that money spigot. If you don't believe me then explain why Illinois is so in debt. How and why did you let it happen? Why did you take off all the locks to your wealth, then let the thieves in and give them the keys to the front door and write down the combination to the safe?

For the sake of the nation and your state, please, please, please take back your authority and kick the bums out. Know who you are voting for! You need to get rid of all liberals and admitted Socialists from all government regardless of party.

While I have your attention I want to encourage you environmentalists to quit being so two- faced. Illinois is blessed with some of the richest black loam soil in America and much of the world. Why then are you paving it over and putting those huge warehouses on such fertile soil? Put permanent borders on all cities and do not allow farmland to be sold to anyone that is not a farmer. Sycamore, why did you put the hospital in the middle of a farm? Environmentalists, shame on you. You didn't say a word. Shame. I don't live in Illinois for many reasons, but the sweet people on the farms and in small towns are not the reason I left.

You don't need to know me and one more time, I'm not important, but my story is. Here is the inside story that is related to Prison Reform. It is now fact that we are a fat society. The Armed Forces solution is called PT, Physical Training. In some schools it is only sports that present this opportunity.

Because of liberal union members, teachers are the same folks that asked my child relative to recite a prayer from the Koran. She refused — bless her conservative little heart — and after Mommy got in the Principal's face she won't ever have to do that again. The same liberal teachers would have had a fit if the teacher had required The Lord's Prayer. Two faced liberals obviously have never read the Koran. It has some social value, but they skip over the mandate to kill anyone that is not a believer, and introduction of Sharia Laws. That book is against our very foundation. Believers should be banned. Why the hell would we elect them to power? America has never been a stupid Country. This is insanity. I am so afraid of what has happened to our schools. I asked a ten year old relative if he reads for pleasure. He said he doesn't read. What?! The teachers are so afraid that he might read any of Samuel Clemens' books or perhaps the wonderful book, To Kill a Mockingbird.

Back to fat people. I don't mean just overweight people, I mean over the belt, haven't seen their privates for years folks. I'm now talking about guards I saw at Pontiac Prison. Yes folks, walking heart attacks that you are going to foot the bill for when it happens. Clogged arteries cost my insurance company $160,000 for a quadruple bypass. Physical standards would keep those folks outside the wall. Why would any employer hire such gluttons? This one's on you, Warden. Who else has informed you folks?

The solution is easy: enforce standards for all State Government employees. Fire the Unions, or privatize and supervise. No retirement expenses. Can you save millions? The answer is yes. Make it happen! Disagree with me at your own expense.

I am not affected by your taxes, but I do care enough about you to stay up all night writing this story. Besides, too many people want me dead. By the time you read this, there will be six books about my case. Four will be the truth, two will be lies. CNN has a big story coming soon that will also be the truth.

CHAPTER ELEVEN
FRIEND BUILDING

I needed to diffuse the tension of those that would do me harm, so I had to make myself valuable. I took compassion on a very strong looking black man. Truly, because he was carrying a bigger burden than all of us. He had prostate cancer and a life sentence for three murders he admitted to. He had no family support and told me he didn't want to live with a colostomy bag and that he hoped to die soon. We walked the track for a long time and I think I lifted his spirits enough for him to put suicide off.

I told him that we were all here for a purpose and he was there for a reason. It may be that he could give others hope. Hope is the thing that sustained all of us. I balanced on the edge of hope as the months turned into years that I couldn't afford to lose.

I knew that once I got back to court, I could get my case reviewed and perhaps a new judge would actually read my FBI files. I had rock solid proof of where I was at the exact time of the kidnapping. I would learn later that I had very powerful people that would help if I could only get back in court. My legal counsel was the best legal mind in Pontiac prison, and he put in a motion that got me before a judge that wouldn't even look at my case. Then I was passed to another judge that threw out my case. Finally, I got a judge that was curious and I would take the prison-road several times.

My case received national attention because it was the oldest cold case in American history to ever go to trial. The attention made DeKalb County nervous. Any honest person with a law degree could instantly see that my case didn't pass the smell test and the prosecution had manipulated the evidence and that the ISP (Illinois State Police) had hidden exculpatory evidence. Then something amazing happened: the original prosecutor lost his election. The new prosecutor put his career on the line. He read everything that had to do with my case, and he found that the timeline did not support the Prosecution's version. He was a brave man that would put his career in jeopardy. He did lose his career. Thanks to him, I am now a free man. Next January the power will be on my side and the Prosecution will be on the stand with the lies turned against them. They are criminals. There are witnesses they can't control, and evidence that they lied to the Grand Jury.

Jeffrey Dean Doty's second book on my case will soon be out, and CNN will release facts that have been hidden from the public for years. The name of my book is You Don't Know Jack. Jeff's upcoming book, co-authored with Dennis Tomlinson, is titled, A Convenient Man. I am the amateur, he is the pro that I admire. His book, Piggyback, may have saved my life from my cellie who had planned to kill me. Like I said, the most dangerous man. Jeff's book, Piggyback, has sales all over the world. The true crime buffs are everywhere, on both sides of both oceans, and they now know that Illinois is the most corrupt state in America and that Chicago is not the "Shining City on the Hill." It is a disaster with more murders annually than any other city in the USA. Perhaps I shouldn't voice my opinion, but the reading public can't refute my words. What they did to an old man and his wife was criminal. Justice is coming, and they won't like what happens next.

When I spoke about education, my favorite hobby has been influenced by my love of the most difficult writing I could find. First I learned Japanese, and now I have four years of intense daily study and a desire to talk with a Chinese language professor.

I also intend to brush up on my Japanese. I spent two years in Japan while I was in the Air Force. I learned to respect the people as a disciplined society with a fascinating feudal history. Even the Samurai were cultured, poetic, and devoted to their master. Honor was a serious matter that could require the ultimate sacrifice for their master, losing face in battle. To our military this could be just another day to rest up, rearm, and resume the battle.

All arts were mastered in depth. The Japanese were perfectionists in all things. I think the discipline and beauty of kanji (Chinese word) that they adopted in the seventh century contributed to the growth of their culture.

Now I will explain why and how language improved my interactions with both individuals and groups. First I will explain why I have such an interest in other countries. I spent a few years as an enlisted Intelligence Analyst. My target at that time was Asia. I became very interested in the Japanese language. I then started to learn the basics of Korean, Arabic, Chinese, Ancient Egyptian and even some dead languages that were the root of modern languages. The motto of Army Intelligence is "Know your enemy." If you don't know something about a country's language and culture you will have consequences.

I was probably the only white person that could read Arabic and had studied the Koran. One day I went up to a black inmate and asked him if I could look at his gold image of a book that had Arabic writing. Then, to his amazement, I told him in Arabic what it said: "There is but one God." Most of the Muslims soon treated me with respect after that.

I met other linguists including a Russian Spy that was fluent in at least six languages. This guy was brilliant, and perhaps the smartest man I had ever met. When he was an active agent, he was a real threat. He was KGB. I learned a lot from him, but he learned nothing from me, I think.

There was another inmate that I respected because he was fluent in Korean and he would pass a Korean newspaper to me for practice. We shared several languages, but he would never be my friend, probably because of my charges which he likely believed. My reason for this story is that you can benefit by using your talent or special interest. All you need to do is find the other folks that share your interests. You need friends to watch your back, so make friends if you can.

Two times a month you will have the opportunity to go to the commissary. Think of it as the bank because you can buy things or favors from other inmates. For instance, I put out the word that I needed a good dictionary, and it only took two days before I was contacted by a guy that had a large heavy American Heritage Dictionary, which only cost me seven Cokes. Not everything was so cheap. When the prison stopped selling light bulbs, the price went up to ten dollars on the black market, the only problem was you didn't know how long it would last. To solve this problem I bought one of those tiny clip on lights. It was adequate, I could still study at night.

It took nine months after leaving prison before I got a good night's sleep. It took about ten years for me to get over Vietnam, but only about four years to get past the stabbing and prison experience. Perhaps writing this book is my therapy. Something good has come from something very bad. My hope right now is that you, the reader, will benefit in some way. If you are better prepared for what is ahead of you, I have done my job. If you are involved with prison reform you have information from a victim of corruption. If you are a voter, this is your heads up to research the folks you elect. You have a responsibility to root out government corruption and let them know who they work for.

I am going to offer this insight that you may or may not agree with. After all, it is only an opinion with one caveat, I spent five years as a law enforcement officer, so I now know both sides of the wall, and what I want you to know is related to a revelation while on the inside. This will sound very liberal from someone very conservative, but I am of the opinion from meeting inmates that the State doesn't need to be, and in some cases shouldn't be, holding for the rest of their lives. I am more inclined to limit nearly all inmates' sentences to seven to twenty years. There are (of course) exceptions; men that will always be a danger to society. That is an easy decision which should be obvious to certain professionals during the inmate's first seven years. Those that fail should be re-evaluated every seven years.

The brilliant minds forever caged on the inside can still contribute to society. The inmate that helped me get back in the court on my road to freedom, Kurtis Williams, is a prime example. I met inmates with degrees, and another Captain (I also had been a Captain in the Army) writing his first book that I'm sure could be an asset. In my estimation, perhaps five percent of the men I met were innocent.

I listened to story after story how an accusation by a wife put their husband in jail. All that needed to be done was to set a court date, book, release and wait for the accused to show up. A no show results in a Failure to Appear, then file an arrest warrant.

Finding someone is almost too easy. I was a police officer on a relatively small department, I decided to pull out the warrants, and then shame some of the wanted individuals into putting the reason for the warrant behind them. They could get an attorney of their own choosing or contact the Public Defender's Office, sign a Promise to Appear, show up, and then face the consequences.

A simple traffic ticket can turn in to a warrant. Defendants don't need to lose their job, get their car impounded, and then lose their car because they are in custody. Poverty should not be the reason for being held in jail, and losing what little they have.

In most cases I would just look in the phone book, call them, and tell them to come in and take care of the warrant. They often moved to hide from their responsibilities. If I couldn't find them, I would just walk over to the city Public Utilities and check the water bill. Viola! An address. Knock, knock. I was also a Deputy Sheriff and delivered folks to my boss for safe keeping. If the new guest of your jail should be evaluated and if he/she wasn't a threat to society, why not just book and release? Ka-Ching! Instant savings. One of the guys I met in jail owned a million dollar business. His court date kept getting pushed back. He was still there when I arrived in prison.

I was convicted by a lie and an incompetent judge, on what must have been the judge's first felony case. He obviously had never read the Constitution. He agreed with the prosecutor to ban FBI reports that proved my innocence. Pure and simple, it was a setup. A conspiracy to convict a man they knew to be innocent.

If all of your accused guests are innocent until proven guilty, why keep all of them? I met one inmate that lost his farm. He was an old guy like me. The charge, being a hoarder.

Sheriff, just sort out who should stay or go. The amount of bail should be flexible. Why do you let dangerous scum walk because they can pay bail with drug money and keep the poor guy that lives paycheck to paycheck? Because money equals freedom? My police Sergeant once reminded me how powerful I was. He said, "You have more power than the President because you could take away a man's freedom." That is you as well, Sheriff, but you have discretion. Please use it.

CHAPTER TWELVE
ASSAULT

Some of what I tell you is emotionally stressful but it is necessary that you are informed so that you can prepare yourself. I'm going to tell you about two events that happened the first month after my arrival at Pontiac Prison which is about a three hour drive from Chicago. I was in Protective Custody and had a bad situation unfold.

I was the second oldest person in a building of eight hundred men. Because of my age and medical condition, I was assigned to the first floor and given a coveted bottom bunk. That was instrumental in a disaster that shouldn't have happened, but the person that assigned it to me placed me in a cell and broke up a relationship between friends.

The next problem was that they took the bottom bunk away from a cool inmate that most of the guys liked. He was a tall, handsome Texan, a mechanic, and had a job maintaining the prison vehicles, which were many and varied. In other words, a valued and talented, even admired, guy. He was also a murderer. He was unfortunately at work, and would return to his cell and find that his friend, a genuinely nice guy, was gone and an old guy had just taken his bottom bunk. Not only that, but I was a convicted child killer and assumed rapist. To him, I was scum and a candidate to murder. Not even two days would pass before he threatened to "slaughter" me.

I take threats by convicted murders seriously, so I told a guard. Now the problem was back in their lap. Like I said, this was a valued and respected individual. I was a problem for the staff, so they needed to move me. I was moved to a single cell which was usually reserved for violent or mentally unstable inmates. That was fine with me, but I was neither violent nor mentally unstable, so another move was directed by the floor Lieutenant. The Lieutenant was a loud mouthed person who should not have the job she did, for she was always yelling for silence in the IDR (Inmates Dining Room). The other Lieutenants knew that this was one of the times to let us talk. She was determined to punish me. That was not her job. She was there to protect all of us, why else would they call it Protective Custody? It became obvious that she wanted me dead, so she assigned me to the guy that she had to have known was going to try to kill me.

An inmate would later tell me that this inmate had told him that he intended to kill me. It was a set up. What happened next became the reason all tooth brushes were confiscated at Pontiac and possibly other prisons as well. Now you will only be issued or allowed a very short toothbrush or a soft plastic brush less than four inches long.

My new cellmate was a short bald cranky hunchback who had a reputation for making trouble. Another inmate told me he was also very lazy and caused others to do his job for him. I didn't even consider him a threat. Don't make this mistake. All inmates are a threat when you are sleeping. Anything in your cell can be used. An extension cord becomes a garrote. Unfortunately for me a sharpened toothbrush became a spike in my right eye.

Now I shall tell you how it went down. On the second day it was shower time, one of our few simple pleasures. If inmates had a job, they could shower every day after work. I think the rate of pay for workers was between thirty five to fifty dollars per month. My guess would be about ten cents per hour. Better than ten dollars per month. After my shower, sometime after noon, I took a nap and fell into a deep sleep. My dream wasn't making any sense because something was hitting my face, head, and ears. I covered my face with my hands but the stabbing didn't stop. Then it happened the toothbrush slipped between my fingers and dented the outside of my eyeball and continued to the back of the eye socket twice. The socket instantly filled with blood which pushed my eye forward perhaps a half inch. I pushed it back in the socket and the blood gushed between my fingers and squirted about six feet, all over my just purchased sweatpants, bed and laundry.

As I sat up, he continued stabbing the back and side of my head cutting my ear. I would have to defend myself with one hand, one foot, and one eye. He had started the attack at the head of the bunk. As I sat up, I rolled over on my right side so that my left leg could kick him.

I said, "What the f--k are you doing? Are you crazy?!!"

The answer came instantly. His face was contorted and his toothbrush was pointed at my good eye. He wanted to blind me. Imagine in prison for life and being blind. That is when instinct kicked in. I kicked him hard with my left foot to his chest. Still holding my eye in with my right hand, I hollered for help. I didn't sound very manly and couldn't get my voice lower than a high soprano. The inmates were all listening but no response. In a fight, they won't interfere.

Then I yelled, "He's stabbing me!"

The guys then made such a racket that the guards came running. He continued the attack, but my hand snatched the toothbrush out if his hand faster than a cobra. Both of us were surprised. I tried to throw it away, but it bounced off the door, and as he bent down to pick it up he was greeted with a flurry of kicks. About five guards were at the door yelling at him to move to the back of the cell, then they came in and grabbed him. All I could say to him was, "You Son of a Bitch", over and over. I couldn't know how I looked but as I read their faces I knew it was bad. My white t-shirt was now red. I didn't know that my cheek was black and that I had lost a lot of blood, but I felt it as I laid back in a puddle on the bed.

The wheelchair arrived and I was on my way out. One hundred inmates were silent. One inmate said two words that summed up his feelings, "Jesus Christ"

I have nothing but praise for all the medical people I would soon meet. The doctor told me to strip naked in front of nurses and several others. I was in shock and did as I was told, but a kind nurse put a prison jump suit over my privates and told me to put it on. The doctor examined my eye. I could only see a very fuzzy image of him.

He exclaimed, "You can see!"

I think I said, "A little."

The doctor forwarded me on to the local Catholic hospital, which sent me on to Chicago for an operation. A bit over two hours later I was on a gurney chained hand and foot. I frightened some people that would quickly walk past. I wasn't a threat, I was a victim.

I don't remember the name of the hospital, but it was a teaching hospital. Perhaps five or six young Doctors introduced themselves. They were there to assist the teaching doctor who would put two stitches in the back of my eye cavity.

A month later I would regain my sight and resume my studies. If you are one of the medical folks that are part of my story and remember me, know that I am so very thankful. You all are very special people. I can't say "God bless you", but if there is a God, may he reward you in this life and in the afterlife, if there is one. Now you know what an agnostic believes. Not very much. (Insert smile here)

The inmate that did this to me died months later, probably by the hands of his cellmate. Paybacks happen. How sad.

I hope that I don't have to repeat this story again. My editor said it was a story that needed to be told, and this was the time and place to do it. Perhaps now I can let it go. I'm alive and well and home with people I love. This will be the best Christmas ever.

CHAPTER THIRTEEN
DISTRACTIONS

So far, I have painted some fairly bleak pictures, so now I want to show some good things I saw and where I saw them. Let me take you back to the yard. The Prison that I was in had two yards; one was small, often a muddy mess in winter and a dusty hot place in the summer. It is important that you know the weather forecast before leaving your cell. Illinois weather usually has four distinct seasons, and I would add that all of them are bad.

The winters are bitter cold. As a boy I sometimes had to push the front door open against snow that was perhaps four feet deep. One winter it was twenty below zero.

Spring is a muddy, but sometimes beautiful experience as plants begin to bud and the world starts to turn green.

In the summer, ninety to a hundred degrees would seem the norm.

Almost all trees in Sycamore are deciduous. In the autumn that meant a trip down Somonauk Street which has old trees that would reach across a wide road in glorious reds and yellow.

Winter made it a scary place; trees with bare branches clawing toward the ice gray sky.

What has all of this got to do with the yard? Only to make you realize how important it is that you prepare because you will have little protection for at least two hours, and it seemed it was always longer when extreme conditions were miserable. We would watch and listen for the big-bellied guard to bellow, "YARD!" Which was our signal to line up by floor and cell group.

At first you won't know what to do because people congregate with people they fit in with. Example: The younger thin guys with excellent hand eye coordination and quick feet would play handball. Watch for a while to see who has talent, and who the winner is. New talent seems to be welcome, so line up and you will have your chance when the guy with the ball screws up. I didn't even know the rules and was too old.

My first goal was to walk. That was where the predators would join you to test your resistance to their agenda. The religious guy may want to recruit you into their prayer group. You might sometimes see a group of guys in a circle led in prayer by that guy. Christians are usually good and kind folks and will welcome you. You could find a friend.

I would rather have a friend that shared a common interest and didn't hate me. To most I was scum. After all I was a baby killer and by extension a probable child rapist. I couldn't remain anonymous. I was world famous. Mine was the oldest cold case brought to trial in American history. Everyone connected with my case was doing high fives and taking victory laps. The problem was they chose the wrong guy. Their turn won't be pleasant.

Besides a healthy dose of fear, your mind will take a beating. I will give you my experiences. If you are going fight for your freedom, be prepared for anguish because you will think about nothing else for years. In my case, I had to search my memory which I later learned leaves out some information and replaces it with new information. This is not just forgetting, it is worse.

Distractions will be your friend when your mind starts beating you up at night. I suggest reading as it is one track thinking that usually doesn't allow deviation from what you are reading. So read to stop painful thoughts such as "Coulda, Woulda, Shoulda." and "If I had only..." I recommend immersion in something that requires focus. I actually slept with several books such as dictionaries in several languages. The guards would often see me studying at night.

Watching TV is how most men deal with self-deprecating thoughts. That only works until you turn the TV off and you are back to your gremlins. For some folks prayer will actually be their salvation as prayer offers the most valuable things, such as hope and forgiveness. Hope will keep you alive, and you must never lose hope in prison.

In a maximum security prison, most of your day will be spent in your cell. Besides your mind, you must take care of your body. Exercise can be performed anywhere so discipline yourself and set goals. Lots of guys are into fitness, so learn from them. At minimum, walk and talk in the yard. I found a coach and took up weight lifting which shows to this day.

I was in the under 200 pound group until one day at age seventy four I benched 200 pounds. I got some respect for that. The guys that were in the 300 club got my respect because they were disciplined and took care of one another. I once saw an inmate lift 440 pounds and saw a one inch steel bar flex like it was rubber. I shall never forget that experience nor the man that did it.

CHAPTER FOURTEEN
PRISON REFORM

I just read a story that indicated that the Governor of Illinois is going to look into Prison Reform. We want action, not words. This is the guy that wouldn't lift a finger to help me. I told him I didn't want a pardon, because I wanted exoneration. All he had to do was to tell his Attorney General to take a look at my case. I guess he was too busy to tell his secretary to make the call. He will get a signed copy of my book as thanks for his actions if he can release the innocent, reduce the length of confinement, and privatize the maintenance and care of prisoners. This would cut out the unions that are sucking away the taxpayers' hard-earned money.

The business people know how to save money, while the government doesn't have a clue, and they forget who they work for. Why do the people keep writing a check for government employees for life? It should be an honor to serve the people. When their term is up, they should find a job like the rest of us do. They are not royalty, they are Public Servants. Their life isn't on the line like soldiers, cops, and the workers they claim to love so much. Imagine a job where you could write laws that allow you to increase your pay, year after year, work for a few years, then retire with full pension until you add even more money when you reach Social Security eligibility.

I have to stop here before the public servants ban this book send the IRS after me.

Without an editor, I could not be an author. For twenty years of my life I carried a gun to protect others. No brag, just fact. As commander of the Fifth Army Honor Guard, I led a parade in downtown Chicago and saluted Mayor Daley Senior as I passed the reviewing stand. Say what you want about him, but he knew how to run a city and most people didn't fear getting shot. They feared him as well as loved him. My point is that guns are not always bad. Strong leaders can be very good, and I did not deserve to spend five and a half years of my life in prison for a crime I did not commit.

Please, voters, go and vote the scoundrels out, not the men of courage such as Richard Schmack, the former State's Attorney of DeKalb County, IL. He put his career on the line to save me. He had FBI proof I couldn't possibly have committed the crime. For his reward you voted out the guy that could have saved your life. Good job folks. Now I ask you to support your Governor and make Prison Reform an accomplishment in his term of office.

Not all prisons are as bad for the inmate as the ones I am describing. I recently spoke to an inmate at a minimum security prison. He had many good things to say about the conditions and freedoms he had.

He described the cells as large and coming with a desk. Not the kind of desk that you may imagine, but a steel surface bolted to the wall and a round stool bolted to the floor, a prized place to sit, read, or write. He spoke about the freedom to leave his cell. He said that he could see the nature that surrounds the prison and how pleasant the view was.

Minimum security prisons are for lesser crimes and people that may be leaving soon. Wouldn't this be a great place to start cutting people loose? Emptying a few of these prisons would save a lot of money for the state. I bet I can tell you why that will never be. Unions.

Why not make a law that all small cells are for one inmate and only large cells can be used for two inmates? Set limits for judges as to the length of sentences they may order. Release as many prisoners as possible and save the peoples' money for better things, like roads, bridges, and public services.

CHAPTER FIFTEEN
IDR

We usually went to the IDR (Inmates Dining Room), twice a day. Each trip could be a danger or just a walk to lunch and dinner. This is the place where you meet new folks, or sit with friends to eat, have a brief chat, and spread rumors about prison staff. No time for chit-chat if you are hungry. You are authorized twenty minutes, but you will get ten. Some of the food we eat is grown near the main building. I heard some of the guys say that guards were getting food from the garden. I didn't see it, but I did know that certain veggies didn't make it to the IDR. Some farmers donate local crops and the State supplies the rest.

During the Olympics we received all of the free Chobani yogurt we wanted. I heard that Chobani lost the contract so much of it was near or just past the expiration date. 'That didn't matter, to us it was a treat we wouldn't normally get.

The cooks would do the best they could to make things tasty. Some meals were excellent because someone was kind enough to donate.

When it comes to food, I would often smuggle food in scalable bags from the commissary. I would load up when the guards weren't looking and risk getting taken to SEG.

That ten minutes was often the highlight of the day. Then, "Back to your cell, your ten minutes is over."

Now a word of caution; the trip to the IDR is not a straight line, so there are opportunities for mischief on the landings. Keep your hand near the rail as you use the stairs and your head on a swivel on the landings. Go with someone you trust. Always know who is near you. Assess quickly friend or foe. I saw a guy get knocked out with one sucker punch. Yep, fat, dumb, and happy just met aggressor.

CHAPTER SIXTEEN
PASSING TIME

To my surprise, I discovered ways to manipulate time (It's only your perception). For example; time will seem to lengthen whenever you are in court, because the judge can push back action on your case, dragging out the arguments for months. It will seem that you are always waiting for the next thing to happen and you just want time to speed up until your next court date. If, however, you learn that your case has been moved up, it may seem that the hours are flying by. This is because it is incumbent on you to get ready with your attorney and you have to rush to coordinate meetings with busy people. Everything will seem to get in your way.

If you are waiting and want the days go faster, do this: Stay awake at night, that's the best time to think. Sleep as much as possible in the daytime. The day will seem to pass quickly, because when you awaken, the sun is going down. Days pass quickly. Want things to slow down? Just get up early and the hours will be filled with things to do, and communication will fill your mind with more things to do. You will be exhausted. Such a long day and here comes another one. Perception trumps reality, you now are the master of time. Don't believe me? Try it.

Another way to speed up your day is take every opportunity to attend events such as church or self-help instruction from well-meaning people. As I remember, commissary day seemed short because it takes time to get one or two hundred men through the line. There were seldom more than four windows for an individual to line up at, then more waiting around for enough men to be marched back with their purchases. Then it's stash them out of site and go to chow, and hurry back to put everything away. I would then separate stuff I got for other folks and make a plan to get my stuff to them (which is forbidden). Another meal and then it is evening TV, then bed time. That was a pretty fast day.

Perception wins again.

CHAPTER SEVENTEEN
CONTRIBUTION

If you are an artist, be prepared to be surprised by the number and talent of some inmates. You will have to find them, so ask around. The guys will tell you who is talented. Almost every human being enjoys being praised for their intelligence or talent. You may have just made a friend. Now you must buy some art supplies from the commissary and prove your talent if you want respect from others.

Money can be a real problem. Many inmates lose contact with family because of rejection caused by the crime they committed. Your comfort food and other small pleasures can make your time easier. The State of Illinois pays inmates ten dollars a month to buy toiletries such as toothpaste, soap, shampoo, or whatever you want. Any other money has to come from the outside, so maintain any relationships you have. Not only for money but your needs for mental/emotional health and stability. Twenty five to fifty dollars will buy your needs and buy you friends (not real friends), favors, or items inmates can get you.

Kindness has its own rewards. Helping others who are desperate people, will win you support that could save your life. You will always need others to watch your back. In the words of Rush Limbaugh, "Don't doubt me!"

FYI, if you are in jail, your Social Security will continue, but if you are convicted, it stops.

The story that I am about to write is information for homosexuals that are headed for prison, but for others, it's information of general interest. When you enter prison, all of your addictions will end. Smoking, drinking alcohol, and sex (other than self-gratification) for most inmates, will end.

Rapists will always be happy to use their cellies. They are known to all inmates, so find out who they are, and avoid any contact. For straight guys, you may be tempted by what appears to be a really beautiful woman, I mean stunningly beautiful boys that have real breasts. Two things will get in your way besides your conscience, and they are, that cameras are everywhere, and the fact that they will have their own cell. I want to help calm the fears of gay guys headed behind the walls. Don't hide that fact that you are gay, just be yourself. You will be protected from predators and you will have your own cell.

There will always be others like yourself. Besides, you will be popular, especially if you have real breasts. All men like beauty. The probability is that you will be fine. Ask for PC when you arrive. Just give a note to the guard in charge of your floor. At Menard Prison, up to thirty men will shower with you. Watch your back. At Pontiac and Statesville you can shower in a single shower. Like Grammy Award winner, Robert Keith (Bobby McFerrin) would say, "Don't worry, be happy."

I am going to take this opportunity to tell on the officers that are in charge of the IDR — Inmates Dining Room. TEN MINUTES IS NOT ENOUGH TIME TO EAT A FULL MEAL! There you go guys, I hope the message gets to the Wardens.

Inmates are supposed to get twenty minutes, but they don't. I would always carry a plastic bag in my back pocket, fill it with food, and hide it on my person and take it to my cell. I think some guards knew, but let it slide because they just wanted to get us back in our cells. Breaking any rule can put an inmate in Seg. For example, passing anything to another inmate is a violation, even a note on a scrap of paper. I even saw a "jerk" Lieutenant send a guy to Seg because the Lieutenant saw a note on the floor of his cell. Someone tossed it in the poor guy's cell as he passed by on his way to the IDR. Thankfully all officers rotate to other areas and Jerk Lt. didn't last long. I don't mean to be disrespectful of officers that have dangerous jobs, but this guy doesn't deserve my respect, he and others will know who I'm talking about.

I'm out and I'm free because I'm innocent. But because I have this unique experience, I have a responsibility to help humanize the inmates and inform the public. I think that this is the right time to make changes. Prison reform is necessary. Like I said before, I'm an agnostic, but if there is a God, I'm sure that He/She didn't put us here to spend our lives locked up. We have given the government too much power, and we must take it back. They no longer realize that they work for us. It is our responsibility to punish corrupt officials, like the ones that took five and a half years of my life, and the lives of many others. Most inmates will never get justice, but all of us must strive to do what we can to change what we can, when we can. This is my contribution, now show me yours.

CHAPTER EIGHTEEN
SEG

When we were in the yard, we would see a handcuffed inmate being taken from the main building with an officer. We would not see that individual for a while as he was on his way to segregation.

SEG is a place of punishment with restrictions on anything pleasant. I don't have personal knowledge because I was a model inmate. I was determined to not stay one day beyond my release date.

One of my cellmates accidently exposed himself to a passing female officer. Without missing a step she said, "Pack your stuff. You're leaving." I didn't see him again for a month.

You will see a lot of gang tattoos. Stay away from the guys with tattooed tears, they are killers.

My inspiration for making prison less painful and more productive is fellow Seattleite, Robert W. Stroud, who became a respected ornithologist. The man that played Stroud in the movie "Birdman of Alcatraz", was Burt Lancaster. Not bad for a man that was in prison for life. He inspired me to make the best of a bad situation and improve my mind.

While in the military, I spent two years in Japan, one year in Korea and one year in

Vietnam. I still can read Japanese fairly well including kanji. I can speak conversational Japanese and read Korean — which is much simpler than Japanese.

While at Menard I learned to read Arabic. While at Pontiac, I learned a lot of Chinese writing and Japanese "Kanji", which means "Chinese word." The Japanese have invented about one thousand new Chinese characters in the last century. An inmate provided me with Korean newspapers which helped me practice reading. I credit my studies for giving me an escape from my environment. If you have self-discipline, you can master nearly anything. Become a master of something. You have the time, make it work for you. Read every book that interests you. A book is your escape, take every opportunity to spend time in the library.

One of the reasons for writing this book is to offer some comfort and advice to make the transition a little less frightening for those newly convicted. I also want to draw attention to the corruption that exists both inside and outside the walls.

CHAPTER NINETEEN
D-DAY

This is not the final chapter, and the story is not over. Yes, I am a free man, but the people that did this to me have yet to face trial. That story is just beginning. When the public learns just how the justice system plotted to imprison a man they knew to be innocent, perhaps then there will be a real investigation into this corruption.

To the public, my message to you is to do something about the corruption before you become a victim of this arrogance. First, vote these people out of office and know who you are voting for when you replace them. You are the gatekeepers, so do your job and keep us all safe. Remind them that they work for you.

These folks have tried to destroy me. They have found people to lie about me. They have manufactured evidence and given false testimony to the Grand Jury. They all profited and enjoyed some fame. Some have retired with a substantial retirement. Some still have their jobs so you, the public, are still in danger from officials that neither know nor care that we have a Constitution. This story is bigger than what they did to me, it is a warning to you.

My freedom is the result of having powerful friends that came to my defense.

Illinois is not my home, so these friends are relatively new. These are the good folks that believe in justice. They never wavered in their defense of me. It took years to correct this injustice. My life was in danger every day of my four years in prison.

The most powerful friend a convict could have would be an attorney from The Innocence Project. Mine is Russell Ainsworth.

My closest friend defended me by finding the truth and making it known to the powerful members of both sides. She is Crystal Harrolle, the Investigator for the Public Defender. She consoled my wife on the internet, and wrote encouraging letters to me while I was in prison.

It took Richard Schmack, the new Prosecutor, to drive the final nail into this injustice. He found and exposed the truth that set me free. He lost his job because of that decision. A true loss for DeKalb County.

CHAPTER TWENTY
MENTORS

In prison you will meet some really smart guys that are improving their minds. Find those guys and make a friend. Become a regular in the library and seek knowledge. Even in prison you will find men of character, wisdom, and talent. Whatever kind of human being that you turned out to be, you will find a match somewhere in your prison. That could be good or bad. Your choice.

You will have a lot of time to waste, enjoy, or put to good use read or study a language or pursue an academic goal. You can also do nothing, gamble, and become useless. That will not attract friends. That will also prepare you for your next job living on the street, should you ever get out.

Learn as much as you can about the inmates that count and determine if you should avoid them or invite them into your pursuit of knowledge. The guy with the biggest dictionary will always beat you at Scrabble. Be that guy. Reference books will help you expand your knowledge and settle debates. Gather as many as you can. Commit to reading every page and mark your progress. Find people that will challenge you. Everyone has a book in them, so plan yours and get started. At least keep a diary of events so that you can reconstruct them later.

You also should pass on your expertise or specialty. The more you help others, the more contacts you can make. Keep in mind that the people you meet in prison can be extremely dangerous. If they are killers, they can't serve more than one life sentence, so what's another life? Seek the advice of others before you commit a mistake you can't fix. Even in prison you can find a mentor that you can learn from. If you can't, then be a mentor to someone yourself.

CHAPTER TWENTY
THE ROOT OF EVIL

I am now going to publicly name all of the people that knowingly imprisoned a man they knew was innocent. The people of Illinois need to become familiar with the people that pose a danger to themselves and hold them accountable. With all of the news on all various media outlets, something should have been done by now. I guess that this whole drama must be completely played out to the bitter end before the voting public realizes that they are the ones in danger. My family and I have already paid a price for the evil that separated us and put me in extreme danger.

This may come as a surprise to some, but the folks that did this to me are still working and have received bonuses and promotions and commendations. Every State in America can be proud of their men in blue for the dangerous job they do, however, Illinois should be ashamed of their State Police. They are hiding the misdeeds of Officer Brion Hanley. Why they would protect a man that would hide evidence and lie to a Grand Jury is curious indeed. Yet that is exactly what they are doing. They claim that the investigation into the death of Maria Ridulph is still ongoing based upon an anonymous tip. On a sixty year old case? Yeah, right!

Then there is the former States Attorney, Clay Campbell, the mastermind who conspired with Officer Hanley to lie to the Seattle detectives (who had no business getting involved). This case is still in the courts, so I won't go into details. I will however give the Illinois voters a picture of the pain and suffering these people caused two old folks.

At this writing I am seventy seven and my wife is sixty four.

When I was arrested, the lies began and didn't stop for years. My wife took over my job and suffered a broken arm doing it. She was alone, and was kept in the dark as to what was happening to me. She managed to keep the job and keep us from going into debt. What began as a lie by a vindictive relative, blossomed into a charge of rape, and a finding of not guilty. Then the prosecution rewrote the actual events of the day that Maria was taken. Add in a hanging judge and you have conspiracy to convict, all while I had proof of innocence that was denied to the court by said judge.

It would take four and a half years and a stab in the eye to get a court date that delivered justice.

I would now like to first address the People of Illinois who are forced to pay taxes to people with a voracious appetite and no respect for you or your paycheck. They will never be satiated.

My reason for writing this is to preserve what I am about to say, because I am addressing people of power. Yes, folks, you the voters are at the top of the list. You must never forget that they work for you. Once in power, they think from the top down. You can and should UN-elect them occasionally to remind them that you are their boss. Now please stay with my message for a few moments while I describe how things are, and how they could be at great savings for you, the top of the chain of authority.

Here is my opinion that only has validity if you agree with me. My credentials are my age, experience, and perspective. I have been on both sides of the wall in positions of great power, both earned and taken. I have been loved, hated, vilified, and attacked. These are the credentials that I hope most of you will never have.

Now, finally, perhaps the solution to some of your problems. I will now speak the truth to power. You, not them. Your military was the only common sense organ that could instill discipline, pride, training, and patriotism into your young men, including myself. Every leader among them is a mentor, responsible for "The Greatest Generation."

Coming from a military background I tend to be less forgiving of anything that shows a lack of commitment. For instance, people from northern Illinois know how to drive in snow. Why then do so many guards fail to show up for work when there is only two inches? I surmise it is because they are not committed. They will stay home and let the working guards do a double shift at increased pay. I also suspect that the unions may be behind this as well.

A sleepy officer among such dangerous inmates as are found in a Maximum Security prison is not a good thing. This lack of discipline should not be tolerated by the Prison or the State. Don't get me wrong, I don't hate the guards. In fact I have respect for the ones that show up even when conditions are uncomfortable to dangerous. Of course, these are not the snowflake liberals. These men tend to have been forged at a more disciplined time. They are the older guys. I have one officer in mind.

He didn't like me much and would yell at me for minor infractions. Truth is I didn't like him at all, but he had my respect because he showed up. A real man that took his job seriously. Only he knows who I'm talking about. Far too few guards are like him. What exactly is the penalty for snowflake guards that put a fellow guard in such jeopardy? I won't get into female guards. This is not the place for Political Correctness. Why is it that a female guard is placed in a guard post that is right in front of the showers? Is the reverse true for male guards in a women's prison? I think not. Did the Warden know about this? I think not. So what's up, Major? I would fire you.

CHAPTER TWENTYONE
JOURNEY

I am not going to try to defend myself against all of the accusations against me invented by people that know nothing about me. I will say that they wasted their time, because I am not a criminal.

They lost the argument when they desperately tried to discredit me in order to win at trial. They actually thought that I would not stand a chance against their brilliant bending of the facts.

Thanks to all of the people that came to my side, the former State's Attorney and his prosecutors may now stand to face criminal charges.

I intended to out all of the bad guys, but I will have to leave that up to the courts. I don't want to make my attorney's job harder.

People will believe what they want, I don't really care. I, as an individual, am not important. So, say what you want, because most of what you have been told is a lie. Soon, the criminal folks will be exposed for what they are, and, hopefully, will be removed from office. My life and time in prison will have served a purpose.

I think that the end of this journey to expose corruption has just begun. The first step of the thousand mile journey has been taken. Even as I write this, the internet has come alive as the story goes national. Several books are in progress. The lies have wilted as the facts got in their way.

It was not pleasant, living out my part in this story, but I would hope that the reader will be better prepared than I was by heeding advice and preparing the mind for what follows. You or they can take some comfort in being prepared. My part is over, but your part is about to begin, and corruption must end.

In the words of John Luc Picard, "Make it so."

CHAPTER TWENTYTWO
RELEASE

The happiest day of my year, April 15, 2016, when I walked, unshackled, out the North Gate of Pontiac Prison. My very best friend was waiting for me. What happened next was an unbelievable act of kindness and generosity. My reason for telling you this is because this could also have been a less than good experience. No one could have predicted that a prosecutor would declare me innocent. I was broke. I don't want you inmates and future inmates to regret not saving money. If you have no one to meet you, you may be back behind bars soon. So be warned, save, save, save.

CHAPTER TWENTYTHREE
SYCAMORE'S PAST

I am now going to tell the seventeen thousand people of Sycamore about a piece of history from the late forties that very few will know. You should be very proud to learn what I have to say, because if the residents ever think that times are rough, I am going to tell you what rough really was to the residents back then when the population was about four thousand. The builders of homes back then were so good that most of the core area houses from the thirties and forties are still there.

Here is a fact from the civil war that I learned as a boy. Just west of Center Cross St. on State St., west of the theater, there are three large stately homes. One of them was part of the Underground Railroad that smuggled black people further north to Canada. I learned this firsthand from the resident that owned the home, a very sweet older woman that lived there. I'm sorry if I cause unwanted attention to the present owner, but it needs to be told. The house is still there, but has been changed quite a bit. Count three houses from Center Cross Street on the south side of State Street going west, and you should see a two story house that once had a cupola on top for observation.

Now back to World War two Sycamore. The forties folks would tell me about how hard life was during the great depression. No wonder these folks were so tough. They would tell me about eating dog food out of a can.

There have been several wars since WWII, but none (except perhaps the Civil War) that so devastated the residents left behind. A tribute to the Civil War veterans stands in front of the courthouse. Sadly, the tribute to the WWII folks was removed during the late fifties. I will now tell you about that wall of names that I was so proud of. Just east of the movie theater, there used to be a small park with a V-shaped sidewalk that led up to this tribute to all the men that served from Sycamore. My Step-father's name was on it, and I was proud to know that he was on the wall of heroes. I learned that if the name had a star on it that the soldier had been killed. There were many perhaps hundreds, that never came home. It wasn't just Sycamore that suffered such loss, it was every little town in America.

Sycamore must find where that monument went and put it in a museum, or recreate it.

To some of the snowflakes that think life is tough now, you should really learn about the history that you are trying to destroy.

I was a Vietnam vet and my tribute is on a wall with friends I lost in combat. There were fifty thousand plus names on that wall. Just to put things in perspective, in World War Two, 400,000 Americans were killed, with up to 50,000 killed in three months during the battle of Okinawa, April 1st through June 22nd (83 days). That is the reason they were called "The Greatest Generation." So now you know, and can really be proud of your town and men that served.

My story tells you what your generation needs to fix before you can be proud of yourself.

CHAPTER TWENTYFOUR
THE FINAL WORD

Before the Illinois State Patrol spends another minute or another dollar, I am going to name Maria Ridulph's killer. That should get their attention. Guess what? His first name actually is Johnny. Speaking as an experienced police officer and a victim of Illinois corruption, I defy anyone to disagree.

Her killer's name is Johnny Hilburn, a Quaker Oats employee from Rockford, Illinois. In the FBI reports Johnny admitted that he was talking to two little girls at six thirty at the corner of Center Cross Street and Archie Place. The only witness left said that, that was the place and time that they met Johnny. He stated that he was asking directions (from seven and eight year old girls) on a street he knew well. He actually spent time in prison (at Statesville Prison) for molesting his five-year-old daughter. He both worked and lived in Rockford, a city on Route 20, the road which also ran right past the patch of woods just outside of Woodbine, IL, where Maria's body was found. Do you think that's a coincidence? I often wondered why the FBI didn't act on such a credible suspect. There is, of course, a reason that involved money. So much money had already been spent by the fifty agents that they just walked away and didn't look back.

Meanwhile, Johnny went on to live out his life and I went to prison for his deeds.

Everything I just wrote is verifiable. It is just time to end this charade and send several state and county employees to the same place where they sent me to get killed. They almost got away with it. I'm still waiting for Justice. I have been cautioned against being vulnerable to a lawsuit. I stand by my words, so bring it. Fair, balanced, and unafraid.

Jack Daniel McCullough

Office of the DeKalb County State's Attorney

DeKalb County
Courthouse 133 W. State
Street Sycamore, Illinois
60178

RICHARD H.
SCHMACK
State's Attorney

General Offices: Tel:
(815) 895-7164
Fax: (815) 895-7101

FOR IMMEDIATE RELEASE

March 25, 2016

PRESS RELEASE

Sycamore, Illinois -

DeKalb County State's Attorney Richard Schmack announced today that he has completed a six-month review of all known evidence in the case of People v. Jack D. McCullough in compliance with a court order to respond to Defendant's Motions. The Answer to the Motion for Relief from Judgment has been filed, along with a Report Disclosing Evidence to the Court and Defendant under Illinois Rules of Professional Conduct 3.8(g) and 3.8(h). Owing to newly discovered evidence undermining the possibility of guilt, and the sheer weight of previously-known evidence, the Answer and Report do not oppose Defendant's motion. Copies are attached to this press release, along with other previously filed materials.

State's Attorney Schmack issued the following statement summarizing his findings:

All reliable evidence obtained from 1957 through today shows that Maria Ridulph disappeared from Sycamore between 6:45 and 6:55 p.m. on December 3, 1957. Almost immediate interviews with her family, friends and neighbors by local, state and federal law enforcement authorities led to this conclusion. At least 20 individuals saw or heard her between 6:00 and 6:45 p.m. and their statements were unfailingly consistent.

2012 trial testimony from Katherine Tessier Caulfield, which appeared to support an earlier disappearance, has been disproved by newly discovered documents. Katherine did not observe police searching for Maria at 7:00 p.m. because 1957 Sheriff's Department documents, as well as FBI interviews with Maria's mother and the Sycamore Police Chief, prove that her abduction was not even reported until 8:00 p.m. Moreover, the 4-H Federation Christmas Party Katherine attended in DeKalb almost certainly ran from 7:00 until 9:00 or 9:30 p.m., and not from 5:00 to 7:00, as she testified, according to Farm Bureau newsletters and the recollections of the 1957 and 1958 Federation Presidents.

The 1957 investigation correctly concluded that John Tessier, now known as Jack McCullough, called his parents in Sycamore collect from Rockford at 6:57 p.m. on December 3, 1957, as has always been conceded by the State Police and the State's Attorney's Office.

74

Illinois Bell records, recently subpoenaed from AT&T, prove that the call was placed from a pay phone in the Post Office once in downtown Rockford, not some other phone booth closer to Sycamore, as had been speculated.

FBI reports show McCullough had contact with Air Force personnel at the Post Office recruiting station between 7:15 and 7:30 p.m. This contact, along with the call from the same building, conclusively prove he was in and around the Post Office from at least 6:55 to 7:20 or 7:30 p.m. that night.

It is a manifest impossibility for him to have been in Sycamore at 6:45 and also have made a phone call in downtown Rockford at 6:57. Even speculating, despite all evidence, that the abduction might have occurred as early as 6:30 p.m., the shortest distance from Sycamore to the downtown Rockford Post Office is 35 miles. Covering that distance in 20 minutes would have required the driver to have averaged over 100 mph for the entire trip on two-lane snow-covered county roads and heavily trafficked city streets in the dark winter night. It is absolutely clear that in 1957, the FBI, the DeKalb County Sheriff's Department and the DeKalb County State's Attorney's Office, properly cleared him of involvement. No mistakes were made by law enforcement or the prosecution at that time.

The Seattle judge who signed the arrest warrant for McCullough in 2011 was grossly misled as to the time of the abduction. The 2010 and 2011 DeKalb County Grand Juries also received misinformation as to the time of the abduction and the timing of Katherine Tessier Caulfield's trip to DeKalb. In upholding McCullough's conviction, the Appellate Court relied heavily on this mistaken testimony from the defendant's sister, and false testimony that there was a streetlight on the corner.

Since McCullough was in Rockford when Kathy Sigman briefly stood on an unlighted corner in Sycamore with Maria's kidnapper in 1957, her selection in 2010 of a black and white headshot of him as a teenager is clearly an unintentional and tragic mistake on her part.

It is well known to professional prosecutors that the identification of strangers from photo arrays, even within a few days of the event, is among the least reliable forms of evidence. It has probably led to more wrongful convictions than any other factor.

Kathy viewed the array 53 years after the fact, and one week after being told there was a new and viable suspect in Maria's murder. The photos were displayed by an officer who knew which photo was the suspect, a practice now outlawed in Illinois. The array was suggestive in the extreme. The other five photos were professional yearbook photos with light backgrounds of young men wearing suit coats. Conversely, McCullough's photo was a snapshot, with a dark background, of him in a shirt with no coat. His was the only photo of someone who lived in Kathy's neighborhood. The others were not even on the FBI's exhaustive list of nearby residents. McCullough lived around the corner and down the block from Kathy, she played with all his siblings and she was a frequent visitor to playmate Johnny Peterson, whose home adjoined the Tessier's unfenced backyard.

In addition, she previously identified someone as Maria's kidnapper. In December 1957, with events fresh in her mind, Kathy viewed a line-up of five individuals. She was able to judge height and weight as opposed to viewing only headshots. She selected a man who was twelve years older and five inches shorter than McCullough. That individual was quickly cleared because he lived in Wisconsin, had alibi witnesses and had only been added to the lineup as a filler.

The Defense was barred from introducing this mistaken identification and evidence concerning another strong suspect viewed in a different line up. She described that suspect as being very close in appearance to the kidnapper. He was also much shorter and older than McCullough. She thought his voice was different though, so although he lived in a nearby town, had a history of child molestation, a witness said she saw a truck bearing his name leaving the scene and his only alibi was his wife, he was never charged. The Appellate Court has since ruled in this case that the trial court's decision to bar this evidence was legally incorrect.

Thousands of pages of improperly excluded police reports more than 20 years old contain a wealth of information pointing to McCullough's innocence, and absolutely nothing showing guilt. This evidence is detailed in a lengthy report which I have filed with the court in accordance with my professional ethical obligation as a prosecutor and my duties as a public official.

I know that there are people who will never believe that he is not responsible for the crime. Many of these people are my neighbors in Sycamore. But I cannot allow that to sway me from my sworn duty to support the Constitution of the United States, the Constitution of the State of Illinois, and to perform faithfully the primary duty of my office, "To seek justice, not merely to convict".

Finally, and on a personal note, I have family and children myself; and truly cannot imagine the pain which this crime brought to Maria Ridulph's family as well as her friends and neighbors. My family has lived for over 30 years in the small Sycamore neighborhood where this crime happened. My children attended West School, just as Maria did.

I truly wish that this crime had really been solved, and her true killer were incarcerated for life. When I began this lengthy review I had expected to find some reliable evidence that the right man had been convicted. No such evidence could be discovered. Compounding the tragedy by convicting the wrong man, and fighting further in the hopes of keeping him jailed, is not the proper legacy for our community, or for the memory of Maria Ridulph.

Acknowledgements

This book would not have been written were it not for the encouragement and guidance of author and friend, Jeffrey Dean Doty. His book, Piggyback, proved my innocence and may have literally saved my life while I was in prison. Jeff is now my editor, my mentor, and my best friend, for always.

I also want to acknowledge the following people:

Richard Schmack, former DeKalb County State's Attorney
Russell Ainsworth, Attorney
Gabe Fuentes, Attorney
Crystal Harrolle, Investigator with the Public Defender's Office
Judge Robbin J. Stuckert
Kurtis Williams, Legal Advisor
Tom McCulloch, Public Defender
Ann O'Neill, reporter with CNN
Casey Porter, my son-in-law, who ran the blog about my case.
Janey O'Connor, my devoted daughter.
Sue McCullough, my loving wife

All of these people contributed to my return to freedom. Each played an important part at various stages of my struggle to defeat the forces of evil. These people are all exceptional in their fields of expertise. One put his career on the line and lost.

And lastly, I have to mention some people from prison. Few people will know who I am referring to, and that doesn't really matter unless you are a researcher that can't stand not knowing. To that person, just enter my name and find me. I will respond if I'm able. I have answered all questions and kind letters to date.

To those that recognize their initials or significant reference, yes it is you, and sorry if I can't remember your name or initials. I'm sure that I will, as soon as the book is published.

OK, J.C., I haven't, nor will I ever forget you. If I ever speak of gambling, I will be thinking of you. When you mentioned your cancer, my heart went out to you, because you quietly carried a bigger burden than most of us. You are a very big and scary guy, but not to me. You were a kind friend when I needed one.

J.H., you were my friend, my coach and protector. You always had my back. When I was with you, I could relax, and just be myself. I was safe. This is so hard to write when I know that I will never see you again. My friend told me that Hemmingway said, "If you don't feel what you write, then your reader won't either." My kind and sweet wife just came to see why

I was so upset (head down sobbing). I just kept saying, "This is so hard!" She understood. You will too J.H. (Sho Nuff)

Now everyone in PC at Pontiac Prison will know who I'm referring to when I say Harry Potter (who was once my celli), because he was so young and handsome. Actually, better looking than the actor. He had a mind like a steel trap. I really envied him, and still do, because I'm good at languages but what took me years to become permanent memory, could be his instantly. So jealous.

About the Author

Jack Daniel McCullough

Born in Belfast, Ireland, the son of an Irish RAF Corporal mother and an English Sergeant father. I was only three when my father died, a victim of German Buzz Bombs. Mother was a searchlight operator at Bovingdon Airfield, NW of London. Like many children during the war, I was placed with a farm family. I lived on a farm near Hemmel Hempstead while mom served her country. The Gates family had a working farm and had little time for a young boy, so from the age of four until six they provided food and a bed under the stairs.

Mom married a Yank who took us to America on the Queen Mary.

It took me several years to mature as I had no social skills. I don't remember ever seeing another child until I was about six.

Sycamore was a great and safe place to grow up, until a neighborhood girl was kidnapped. This is where my story begins and years later comes back to almost get me killed.

If I told you my life story from December 3rd, 1957 until April 15th, 2017 you probably wouldn't believe me. The biggest influence of my life was my time in service. I progressed through the ranks at an unbelievable speed once I joined the Army. I began as a PFC intelligence analyst and ended up an Infantry Captain. The Vietnam War was a factor. Also being at the right place at the right time played an important part as rank came quick to those that served in combat.

After the war I became a police officer, and later a photographer. I also started a successful transportation business with my wife, Sue. We later were semi-retired and living in an apartment complex — I worked the night-time security there. This is where my life entered the rabbit hole: the unbelievable story of government corruption that is still ongoing today.

CPSIA information can be obtained
at www.ICGtesting.com
Printed in the USA
FSOW04n0717021017
39399FS